Seoul.

Standing in t[...] to believe that up until 1950 [...] capital's fate was still uncerta[...] dynastic kingdom to Japanes[...] this is a city that's worked hard to get to where it is.

Which isn't to say that all tradition has been lost. The streets of Seoul boast some of the world's most exciting eating, while its temples and cultural spaces are a haven for contemplation and mindful consumption. While the almighty Michelin Guide has begun to infiltrate Korean food culture, the mavericks behind the city's most creative kitchens and artistic studios, blending local customs with global sensibilities, have already been acting as de facto ambassadors.

Seoul is home to a fascinating set of restless spirits, grappling with all this recent growth and bringing their own tradition into a globalised 21st century. We spoke to an acclaimed artist who blurs the line between art and object and a fashion designer redefining the notion of "classic", a food critic in love with his country's cuisine and a DJ who grew up along with the local underground scene. The city is rife with niche boutiques, music bars and artisan showrooms breathing new life into former indus- trial spaces. The buzz is palpable—and there's never been a better time to get lost in Seoul.

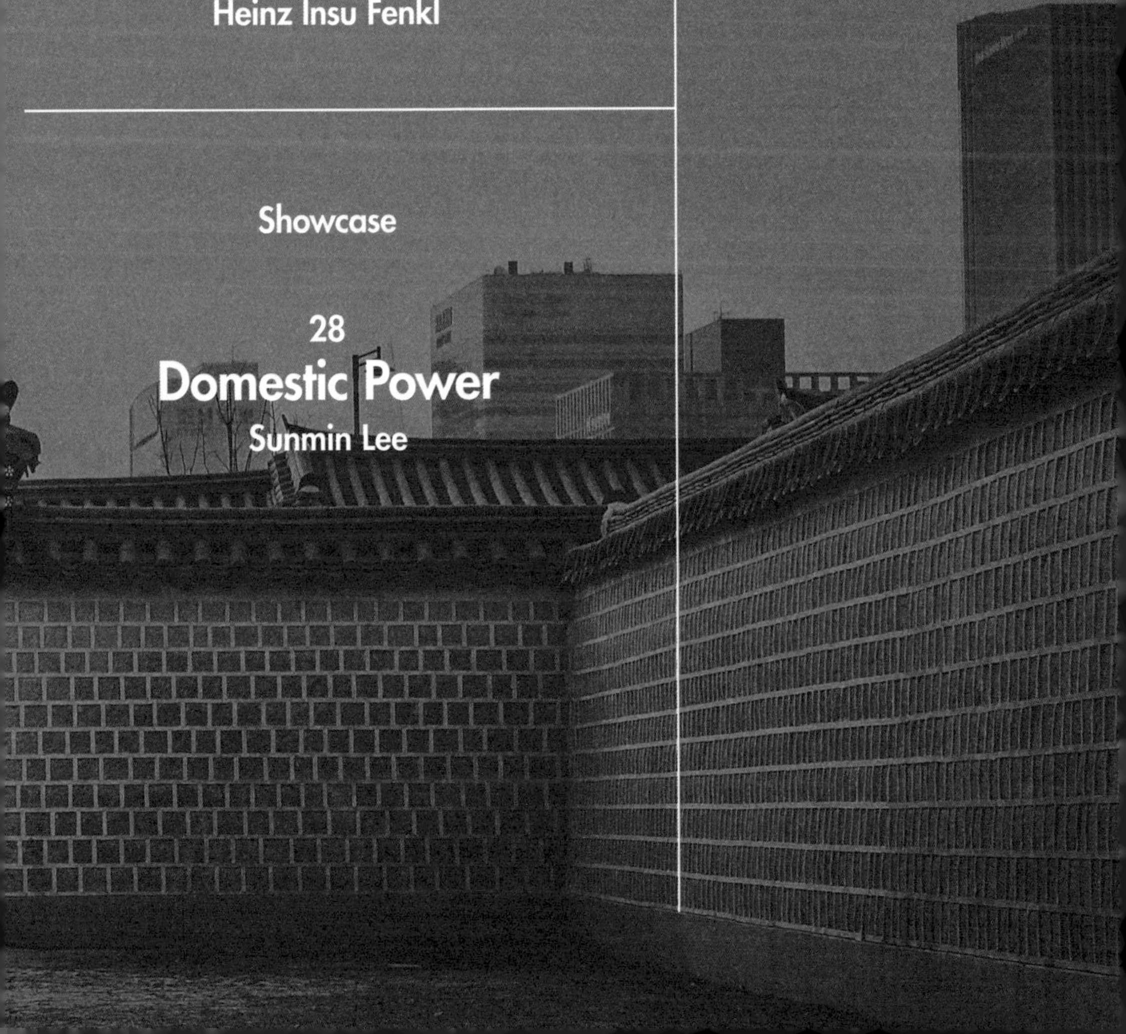

Buk Seoul Museum is a natural and cultural oasis within a sea of residential high rises in the city's north-east. Designed by Samoo Architects & Engineers as open-air affair for contemplation and community, its landscaped walkways cut across the terraced Nowon hill, so a leisurely stroll amongst sculptures and greenery segues seamlessly into an art viewing. A rotating programme features family-friendly interactive exhibitions by renowned Korean artists like Hyun-mi Yoo and Jackson Hong. Admission is free and the campus include a café and shop.
• Buk Seoul Museum of Art, 1238, Dongil-ro, Nowon-gu

Royal Contemporary

South Korea's National Museum for Modern and Contemporary Art, known as MMCA, is a multi-campus institution offering some of the region finest emerging and world-renowned works by Asian artists. The Deoksugung location, whose archive comprises mainly of Korean art spanning 1900 to the 1960s, poses an extra advantage—it's located within a cultural landmark palace.
• MMCA Deoksugung, Sejong-daero, 99, Jung-gu

From Private Booths to Flowers with a View

Light Speed

Safe Haven

This multipurpose arts and cultural centre was dreamt up as a beacon of creativity in a city where development is picking up speed. Rotating exhibitions span disciplines and mediums, with recent shows dedicated to award-winning composer Ryuichi Sakamoto and British designer Jasper Morrison. The complex also houses a café, shop, gallery, pop-up spaces and a Michelin-starred farm-to-table restaurant named Zero Complex. *Noramdaemun* market, across the street, offers a slightly more democratic eating experience.
• Piknic, 194 Namchang-dong, Jung-gu

| Soldiering On

Historically Seoul's most international neighbour-hood—with a close proximity to the U.S. army base—Itaewon has always fit the bill for the type of diverse and slightly edgy neighbourhoods that make for good nightlife. It's no wonder, then, that a concentration of some of the city's most entertaining after-hours options are found here. Take *Queen*, the raucous sweatbox that reigns supreme on the local LGBTQ+ circuit and is favoured by patrons both queer and straight. *Beton Brut* is aesthetically more sober, with a rotating lineup of local house and techno heroes. To keep the rhythm going, hit up the DJ-run *Deviate*, where sixth-floor bay windows and a solid programme will have you dancing to acid house and disco edits until the sun comes up over Itaewon... or until you pop over to *Against The Machine*, better known as ATM, another turntable-equipped venue whose low-key status has made it popular among local celebrities.

• Various locations

Epic Legacy

Housed in a complex of structures designed by María Botta, Jean Nouvel and Rem Koolhaas, the Samsung Group-backed *Leeum* is not one for small gestures. The museum's name is derived from the late Lee Byeong-cheol, former president of the Samsung Group, and was created to display both his jaw-dropping personal collection as well as an impressive array of domestic and international artists, both emerging and renowned. From traditional Korean arts and crafts to the most avant-garde contemporary creations, to a cultural centre made especially for the little ones, this is a a cultural one-stop shop.

• Leeum, 60-16 Itaewon-ro 55-gil, Hannam-dong

Belt It Out

No true Korean night out would be complete without a stop at a noraebang. Between the mandatory pauses for pork belly grilling and soju drinking, it's hard to go wrong with any noraebang joint you happen upon, but, *Su Noraebang* offers the added plus of transliterated lyrics. So you can sing along in a well-lubricated fashion to all your new favourite K-pop songs.

• Su Noraebang, 67 Eoulmadang-ro, Mapo-gu

Outdoors **Green Dream**

No matter how much you might enjoy pushing through hungry daytime throngs to procure lunch, or nighttime crowds to get down in a concrete-clad techno bar, everyone needs a break from the city sometimes. And in Seoul, that break is called *Hangang Park*. This river-adjacent boardwalk and green lung offers a welcome respite from the urban din. Regroup while cycling or walking its quiet paths, or choose from the ample selection of benches from which to take in city views and the equally dazzling Han River. Late summer sees the park's fields explode with colour thanks to the blooming cosmos flowers, a fuschia spectacle to behold all its own. Bikes and swan boats are also available for rent.

• Hangang Park

Shop **People of Print**

Part of a larger cultural centre called Sounds Hannam, *Still Books* is the chapter dedicated to all things paper and letters. From big-publisher titles to more obscure and independent publications, the store manages to please bookworms both mainstream and niche. A different monthly theme sees the whole shop's selection change to accommodate a new theme—a selection that includes Still Books-branded products and items made in collaboration between shop owners MAGAZINE B and other brands. The space also serves as a venue for workshops and seminars.

• Still Books, 35 Daesagwan-ro, Hannam-dong

Hyemee Lee
She's the brains and heart
behind fashion label EENK,
a successful local brand that's
received more than one recent
mention in international gloss-
ies as one of Korea's houses
to watch

Hyemee Lee, Fashion Designer

Social
Fabric

From the clean lines of her timeless separates to the falling leaves
in her neighbourhood's landscape, Hyemee takes in and creates
through shape and colour. Here, the designer extols the virtues of
a life unplugged and shouts out a local hero or two

How did you get started in design?

I had a talent for art from as early as kindergarten years, but I couldn't decide whether to major in design or art because of my conservative family environment at the time. I was also interested in science, so I chose to major in engineering when I first entered university. While struggling with computer science, I was really impressed by my roommate who was majoring in design at the time, so I decided to change my major to textile and clothing design. I didn't plan anything in detail, it just happened naturally, and I guess it eventually worked out. Looking back on it, I was following my instinct and I feel like it was all meant to be.

When did you realise you wanted to do fashion?

When I was in my teens. My mother was into art and fashion, so my sister and I always had unique outfits and I think it translated into a special sense of style. We used to get a lot of attention from people growing up because of what we'd wear. As I got older, I took the lead and honed my own taste. I often went out of town to find new pieces and search for things that I wanted to wear. I started to feel the desire to make my own clothes around that time.

What is your relationship with Seoul?

Seoul is my offline social network. The space where I started design and where I meet my friends, partners, muses. It's where I build on my relationships with all these people—where we share information and inspiration. It's a very social city.

How does the city influence your work or your designs?

Seoul is such a contrasting, eclectic city. It's conservative and very trend-driven at the same time, personal and collective, where both digital and analog preferences are all mixed together. My work is based on classic design and I tend to add something new, while trying not to set limits to an item or a design. I think that part has been influenced by the colour and the atmosphere of the city. Also the heart of Seoul is its people. Seoul friends and family are definitely my greatest source of inspiration.

If you had to design the perfect piece for Seoul, what would it be?

I would design a unisex v-neck knitted cardigan in a classic silhouette with unique details. It could be worn as a top and also as an outerwear piece. It would be more formal than a t-shirt and more active than a jacket and suit any place and occasion, all hours of the day or night!

What are some of your favourite places to go shopping for home decor?

MK2 Showroom is where I find lots of vintage furniture and *Informalware* always has a very well-curated selection of unique lifestyle items. *Orer Archive* is also one of my favourites. It feels like peeping into a collector's work-room. Now that online shopping and social media are so evolved, it's easy to find anything on the Web, making it unnecessary to really go around looking for something new. But finding these thoughtfully selected pieces in these inspiring spaces is always so motivating.

Is there good vintage clothing shopping in Seoul? If so, where would we find it?

My favourite vintage den closed a few years ago, so now I often go to *Gwangjang Market*. I love shopping at well-organised vintage shops, but the sheer joy of unearthing hidden

Orer has a whole floor dedicated to antiques—an experience that feels like peeking into a collector's workshop

Gwangjang Market
Jongno-gu

treasure is something only a market can give you. It's divided into shops; the relatively younger generations are running stall-like shops, operated by older shopkeepers. Finding treasure in those stalls is so much more satisfying for me. It's also a personal dream of mine to open a well-organised, archive-like vintage shop in Seoul so people can come and feel like they're in a museum.

Are there any other fellow designers whose work you really admire?
    BMUET(TE) is a ready-to-wear label created in 2012 by designers Byungmun Seo and Jina Um. They mix and match materials, work with experimental silhouettes and are generally very unconventional when it comes to constructing garments. The brand is definitely a unique concept, they are rulebreakers. They've gained international

awareness recently with their menswear, and they've just branched out to womenswear. Our showrooms are actually side by side, so they're perfect tripmates for global fashion weeks, and we are always exchanging advice. Even if we weren't friends, I'd still be so impressed with the way they've managed to stay unique and beautiful in such a trend-driven city like Seoul, and for managing their hectic schedules so professionally!

Where in the city do you always find inspiration?
    Namsan Sowol-ro—where our showroom and office are located. It's where I spend most of my time throughout the year, and the scenery always has an inspiring and healing effect on me. The colour of the leaves as the season changes, it's beautiful. Another place is

Dongdaemun Market. I've been coming to this market ever since I started to design, and yet I still find something new every time I visit. Even though I could find everything I needed online, I believe the raw, elementary materials need to be seen and touched. You have to see everything through to completion. It's definitely a must, every time I go there's always something new to see, find, study.

If someone is visiting you from abroad, where do you always take them?

For someone looking for modern Korean cuisine, I can recommend *Gebang Sikdang* and *PARC*. But if you're looking for a more contemporary and still sophisticated taste of Seoul, I'd say *Minu.c* for killer seafood and meat, *Gnocchibar* for amazing Italian and *Tamarind* for delicious Vietnamese food with a contemporary feel. Afterwards I'd take you to *Photomatic* for a fun portrait memento of Seoul!

Who makes your favourite comfort food?

My husband makes me food with all of my favorite ingredients. He takes care of my health—more than I do—and always prepares a special dish at home the day before I leave the city for a business trip. After he realised that I really enjoy clean meals with rice, he started a rice business and now it's become his own brand! Besides the fact that he always uses the flavours that I like, knowing how much effort and devotion he puts into it always touches my heart and makes the mealtime a happy moment.

Any favourite bookstores or art supply stores? What makes them special?

I always collect design magazines from *Paper Muse*. For me it was love at first sight, when I saw all the foreign design titles on display. When I visit other cities, I always try to find a small bookstore that represents the spirit of the city and its scene, and I bring one book back. In Seoul, that place would be Paper Muse. It's always comforting to know that my wishlist of publications is in their selection.

You work with artists for a lot of the motifs in your collections—are there any art galleries you like or any particular artists whose work you really admire?

I'm lucky to have great galleries like *Piknic* and *Whistle* in my neighbourhood, so wonderful contemporary art is always just a step away. Recently I've also been seeing a lot of interesting art and design at Cava Life, an online platform that features artists from different backgrounds in art, design, furniture, photography, ceramics, video art and more. They also operate pop-ups occasionally. Additionally my friend, painter Min ha Park, is kind of like my personal liaison between art and fashion. My recent collections drew a lot of inspiration from my studio visits with her. We collaborated by applying her paintings on some of EENK's pieces. And I'm currently working on my next collection, inspired by choreographer Yanghee Lee. Interacting with artists from different fields is always exciting.

A view from Jiieh G Hur's "Electric Smash", shown at the inspiring Whistle Gallery

Euljiro & Jongno

Urban Oasis

Most of the bars, cafés and clubs that moved to this former industrial district have made a point of preserving original façades—lending an even more credible air of cool to the party-ready neighbourhood

| Food | Pigging Out

Are you paying attention? Good. Then head to Jongno-3-ga station's exit six and find the tiny street that leads to a fork. On arrival, the aroma will hit you. Grilling pork is part of the Korean identity, and all throughout the year you'll find locals flocking to this network of alleys after work to grill and share soju shots with friends and colleagues. This boisterous pork belly alley has been a beloved spot for decades. Narrow pathways get even tighter as some two dozen restaurants set out plastic tables and chairs to accommodate the throngs of customers. The right way to eat Korean barbecue is by making a ssam: using lettuce or perilla leaf to cradle your meats, condiments, kimchi and steamed rice. The result is delicious and endlessly customisable. Thanks to a constant circulation of patrons, ingredients in most of the joints here are fresher than your average Seoul pork restaurant. The area starts to wind down around 10 p.m., or whenever vendors sell out. When that happens, head around the corner to one of the few remaining red-tented pojangmacha stalls for another round of rice wine and snacks.
• Pork Belly Alley, starts at 7 Donhwamun-ro 11ga-gil

In Dialogue

Tucked away near the Jongmyo Shrine on a quiet one-lane road lies *Ida*, a three-storey establishment serving up Korean cuisine with a decidedly contemporary twist. Or is that contemporary cuisine crafted with traditional, seasonal Korean ingredients? To help you decide, a field study of dishes like galbi and purple corn grits, sea urchin rigatoni and regional bitter greens doused in gochujang oil should offer some insight. Topped off with homemade popsicles in exciting flavours, this is one conundrum that perhaps needs no solution.
• Ida, 141-5 Seosun ra gil153

Food **Down to Earth**

Call it globalisation, zeitgeist or just the power of the bean, but one thing is for certain— Koreans are crazy about coffee. So much so that you'll find it brewing in the most unexpected places. Like the tiny Euljiro alleyway, wide enough for one, where *Coffee Hanyakbang* has set up shop in a former herbal apothecary. Paying homage to the 16th-century Korean doctor who used to operate out of it, this café still features special cabinets for herbs, as well as lacquered chests and on-theme artwork.
• Hanyakbang Coffee, 16-6 Samil-daero 12-gil

Shop **The Mothership**

Once an electronics megamall populated with shops that carried everything from cables and motherboards to discrete recorders and porn, *Sewoon Plaza* is a cult favourite with a seedy past. A renovation in 2017 introduced a footbridge to connect its seven different buildings, and a handful of galleries, bars and cafés quickly followed suit. The dated gadgets are still there, but now you'll find them on your way to places like *Horangii Coffee* with its top-notch brews and fruit sandwiches, or gallery-cum-artist-studio *Saen Art Space*.
• Sewoon Plaza, 159 Cheonggyecheon-ro

| Shop | **Back to the Future** |

Time travel to the 1990s via *Cosmos Wholesale*, where all things random and nostalgic are packed into every nook of the store. From VHS tapes of old Hollywood hits and holographic stickers, to novelty keychains and printed glass cups, this boy band-era repository has grown exponentially since its five founders dug up their prized collections of tween paraphernalia. Independent bookstore *Normal A* (pictured) offers a slightly more serious browsing experience. Run and curated by a design duo, the naturally-lit shelves feature an exciting selection of magazines, comics and design books.
• Normal A, 2F, 121-1 Euljiro

| Food | **A Second Life** |

Once frequented by neighbourhood workers eager to gulp down cheap beer and nibble on dried fish after a long day, Nogari Alley is now a young locals' favourite. In warmer months, the eateries that dot the area spill out into the alley-ways via those iconic red and blue plastic stools. *Myeongdong Golbaengi* is a great place to drink cheap draught beer from hefty half-litre glasses after dinner. Even after a hearty barbecue dinner, Koreans like to eat with their drinks, so make like a Seoulite and order the sweet and spicy rice cakes with seafood and savoury pancakes—fried to crisp perfection.
• Myeongdong Golbaengi, 14 Chungmu-ro 9-gil

| Night | **Top to Bottom** |

With drab '70s—era buildings nestled between newer, shinier structures, Euljiro is definitely a nightlife destination in disguise. Those who look closely are rewarded with a smattering of places plying their own unique version of nocturnal fun. *Seendosi* is one such quirky bar and impromptu cultural centre with a name that references the area's gentrification. Their hodgepodge selection of furniture includes bus benches, a winking reference to the bus line offices occupying the building's second floor. Drop in on a weekend night to find the room abuzz with kitschy lighting, local DJs and dancing Seoulites.
• Seendosi, 5F, 31 Euljiro 11-gil

20

Culture | **Higher Power Hour**

Most Buddhist temples in South Korea are hidden within the mountains—a remnant of the Confucian Joseon Dynasty's oppression of other religious practices—, but *Jogyesa* is a shining exception. This temple is the main place of worship of the Jogye Order, Korea's largest Buddhist organisation. Nestled within the centre of Seoul, it offers both believers and curious visitors alike the chance to take a break from the bustle of the concrete jungle. Accompanied by a higher power, or not, practice some deep breathing in between the traditional palaces that dot the grounds and snap some respectful photos of the colourfully photogenic details. If you're lucky, you might catch a glimpse of a traditional ceremony. For those in search of a bite-sized spiritual experience, try a three-hour temple stay to learn about Buddhist etiquette and share tea with a monk (reservation required).

• Jogyesa Temple, 55 Ujeongguk-ro

Some trips
for bad

re too short meals.

Make sure they're
all good with the LOST iN app.

Living Food
What a British Food Critic Doesn't Know About Korean Food
Jieun Choi

Arguably the most reputable restaurant guide in the world, the Michelin Guide is a matter of life and death for some seasoned chefs. Earning a star not only drives hundreds of eager gourmets to the restaurant, but also vests the chef with a sense of accomplishment. The debut of the Michelin Guide in Seoul last November, therefore, signaled that the South Korean gastronomy scene was on a par with countries that have longer pedigrees of fine dining, like France and Italy.

A total of 24 restaurants in Seoul were given at least a star, 13 of them serving Korean cuisine. Two Korean restaurants were given the highest denomination of three Michelin stars: *Gaon* and *La Yeon*. Many South Koreans, known for their obsession with promoting Korean cuisine overseas, welcomed the stars enthusiastically. But some critics had misgivings about Michelin's generosity.

One of them was British food critic Andy Hayler, who claims to have eaten in all the Michelin three-star restaurants in the world since 2004, including in *Gaon* and *La Yeon*. Much to Hayler's consternation, his visits to the restaurants, which should provide "exceptional cuisine that is worth a special journey" (Michelin's definition of three-starred restaurants), were less than satisfying.

According to Hayler, despite the good ambience and excellent service, the food itself did not stand out compared to the Korean food he ate elsewhere — mostly places with big Korean migrant communities, like Los Angeles, Tokyo and New Malden in London. In an interview with *Korea Exposé*, he admitted that he is no Korean food expert, but asserted that this does not disqualify him from distinguishing the remarkable from the good.

He pointed out the ingredients that fell short of the high standards that Michelin usually holds. Standard ingredients like beef, chicken and seafood were "fine" but not exceptional. To Hayler, what Korean cuisine really lacks — in general, not just at *Gaon* and *La Yeon* — are luxury ingredients like white truffle. "Can you compare kimchi to risotto with white truffles? Certainly not," he said. "There are some limits to what you can really do with some pickled garlic or pickled cabbage."

Hur Jae-in, co-founder of *GBB Kitchen*, a Seoul-based cooking studio, and a gourmet who has dined in at least 150 Michelin-starred restaurants worldwide, said Hayler's assessment of Korean cuisine is narrow-minded.

"Of course you can't compare white truffle risotto with kimchi. Truffle is a delicacy that goes well with any dish. Of course people would instinctively feel that [the truffle's] umami flavour is more appetizing than the sour kimchi," she said."There are so many different types of kimchi. The flavours change depending on who is making the kimchi, and how much the person uses the different spices, the salts, the type of salted seafood, etc."

Hur said that a "perfect mathematical formula" exists for a white truffle risotto, which not many chefs have the technical expertise to master, whereas there is no textbook answer for kimchi, the taste of which is more a matter of preference. Even South Koreans can't identify the "perfect kimchi." It's possible — and likely — for people to prefer kimchi from a small bibimbap place in a village nowhere, than the ones served at Gaon and La Yeon.

But another Korean food expert, who asked to be identified only by his surname Park, said that South Korea does lack fine and rare ingredients because ingredient varieties are limited by the country's small and relatively homogenous landscape. The overall dry climate, save torrential downpours in the summer, stymies abundant growth of flora and fauna. Many ingredients in Korean cuisine originated from abroad, including a main ingredient for kimchi, red pepper, which originates from Latin America and is thought to have been introduced to Korea through Japan in the late 16th century.

Like Michelin inspectors, British food critic Hayler might have been similarly misinformed about Korean cuisine. Invoking his experience with French cuisine, Hayler bemoaned the level of technical prowess at Gaon and La Yeon, and by extension doubted the technical capabilities of Korean cuisine in general. He found Korean desserts rather simple, compared to French pastry, which calls for hours of preparation and years of mastery. He also equated the absence of an "elaborate French sauce like demi-glace" to an absence of technical skill.

But this, for Hur, shows Hayler's lack of understanding. "Making traditional Korean sauce, like soy bean paste and red pepper paste, takes a lot longer and requires professional skill," she said, adding that the purpose of fermentation was not only for the taste, but also for preservation, which is not the case for demi-glace.
But Park and Hur think the inspectors still lacked proper understanding of traditional Korean cuisine, which is innately different from French and Japanese cuisines. What the inspectors overlooked is that traditional Korean cuisine serves a number of dishes at once. "Traditional Korean food is not a 'dish.' Instead, sundry side dishes with rice and soup are served altogether on the table. The 'dish' is created inside one's mouth, by combining the different foods. So each person has a different experience even when he or she shares the same table with others," said Park.

And traditional Korean cuisine is not served à la carte, which means it is difficult to recreate a fine dining experience, almost always served as table d'hôte — a multi-course meal — in the West. Hur said she had not been to either of the three-starred restaurants in Seoul, precisely because of her unfamiliarity with and bias against traditional Korean meals rendered in a course format. "Even kings did not eat a course meal in Korea," said Hur. Over the years, the Michelin Guide has been criticized for being biased towards French and Japanese cuisines. Last year, Japan had the most number of three-Michelin-starred restaurants, 32 to be exact, and France had 26. While the Guide withholds its exact assessment criteria, it highlights the importance of ingredient quality, techniques, originality, value for money and consistency in execution.

Since 2009, the South Korean government has spent millions of dollars introducing Korean food to the global audience. The efforts of the "K-Food globalization project" included creating a top-tier Korean restaurant in Manhattan (which was never realized), publishing cookbooks in multiple languages and setting a taskforce to with K-Food on UNESCO's intangible cultural heritage list. Over the past eight years, Korea's Ministry of Agriculture, Food and Rural Affairs spent 153 billion won (135 million dollars) on the project alone.

Michelin's ad revenue from the Korean government doesn't necessarily mean the Guide was biased more favorably toward Korean restaurants. The Seoul Guide has certainly helped the government's K-food promotion, but it has also had unintended consequences. Gaon and La Yeon's three stars are fuelling debate about whether they deserve the acclaim, whether Korean food meets the Michelin criteria, and whether Michelin understands Korean cuisine.

Hur Jae-in is not too concerned. "The inaugural Michelin Guide need not be the correct answer," she said. "Even in New York City, where competition is more fierce, the number of Michelin stars changes every year. Think about how many of South Korea's stars would change in the future."

Jieun Choi is a photographer and journalist who covers politics, society, the art world and food. She has worked in Seoul and Melbourne.

Domestic

Power

A showcase by
Sunmin Lee

An observation on
Korea's fraught
relationship with
gender roles takes Lee
to the stage where
both struggles and
victories unfold—inside
the home. What
follows is an excerpt
from her expanded
series 'A Woman's
House.'

Hyunsub Song
He's a house & techno DJ who cut his teeth at a local hotspot for underground club culture. These days, he hosts monthly parties featuring colleagues from all over the world in various venues throughout Seoul

Hyunsub Song, DJ and Promoter

Four to the Floor

Soft-spoken but deeply passionate about his city's nightlife scene, Hyunsub waxes poetic on the legendary local nightclubs that inspired him and where he takes visiting friends when the lights turn back on

Where do you live in Seoul? Is it the same area you grew up in? What is it like?

I was born and raised in Uijeong-bu, a satellite city northeast of Seoul. It used to be a military base for the U.S. garrison, though most are gone now. Compared to Seoul centre, it's relatively peaceful and green. I get good energy from this area.

What's your relationship with your city?

Growing up so close to the American troops, we were exposed to more Black music and culture. I remember enjoying going to the fairs on the army base. Uijeongbu is quite mountainous—just a short drive away from forests and temples. I still enjoy spending time alone in places like these.

What was your first experience with clubbing in Seoul?

Out of curiosity, I went to the "Cola-theque" parties, which were dance clubs for minors that served non-alcoholic drinks. And then nightclubs, which mostly had a strong emphasis on hookup culture, not really music-oriented. My first authentic clubbing experience came in my early 20s when I visited Matmata, a small underground club in the Hongik University district. It's the club that introduced Seoul to Derrick Carter, and there they played house music, not Eurodance or K-pop. To this day, Matmata is still one of the places that's had the biggest effect on me.

What are some of your favourite local record stores?

I would say *Clique Records*, without a doubt. The store is run by a couple of friends with a deep knowledge of music. They've been keeping it up for over four years now—not an easy feat in an environment like this one, where

demand is scarce. The diversity and the quality of the collection here is proof of their affection for and devotion to music. I believe that just by existing, Clique has had a positive influence on the local scene.

You host a lot of visiting DJs and friends who come for weekend visits. Where do you like to take them for a traditional Korean hangover-cure breakfast?

There's one great place called *Byeolnaeog*, they do beef soups and short rib stew with all the side dishes. It's open 24 hours and is perfect for the middle of the night or the morning after.

And any favourite bars to get into the partying mood?

Against the Machine, near Euljiro, is a great place for a drink and some snacks before going out. And there's another venue called *Concrete Bar*, which looks amazing and has a big sound system. We used to host an after party there.

Are there any places we can still go to experience underground club culture in Seoul?

Personally, I don't think any club has been able to fill the space left after Mystik closed. But there are definitely some underground clubs putting a lot of effort into their programming based on that philosophy—places like *MODECi* and *Trippy*.

From Itaewon's underground dens to the student bars in Hongdae, the Seoul nightlife scene is as robust as it is varied

Nerve Centre

Since the city's urban planners connected it to the rest of Seoul in the 1980s, Hongdae has become home to the local bohemia—and their corresponding ventures

Night	Round and Round

From yesteryear's teen idols to the latest in North American folk rock, Seoul's LP bars offer something for every taste—with clientele as varied as the records themselves. Time seems to have stopped at *Suzie Q*, the quaint basement bar run by an elderly couple. Scribble your song request on a piece of paper and wait to hear it while you munch on complimentary popcorn. If you're looking to get a head start on the night and have a craft beer hankering, stop by *There There*. Run by a former music writer, this one's all about western rock and pop—with a drinks list featuring cocktails named 'Oasis', 'Blur' and 'Get Lucky'. *Gopchang Jeongol* (pictured) hits closer to home by way of an epic collection of old school K-pop. Get your boogie on with the locals (and sing along if you can) underneath the neon lights. Once you've worked up a hunger, grab a plate of tofu with kimchi or any of the savoury pancakes.
• Various locations

Handmade Tale

Object's three-and-a-half storey building stands out amid the red-bricked residences of its neighbourhood. Their philosophy of conscious consumerism and environmental friendliness is evident in their array of upcycled and handmade items. Products from over 100 local designers run the gamut from stationery and plushies to clothes and accessories, and it might take hours to browse through all the thoughtfully curated items in the brightly-lit store. Don't just grab a new phone case for yourself—buy a handful of postcards, go downstairs, order a coffee with dessert and write letters to those you love back home.
• object, 13 Wausan-ro 35-gil, Seogyo-dong

Food | Bean Around the World

As much an industrial chic celebration of coffee culture as a welcome respite from the din of the streets, *Anthracite Coffee* is ideal for those looking to power up and quiet down in a worldly setting. The building, a former shoe factory, still boasts many of its original details—now accompanied by ambient music and the aroma of roasting beans. For a more traditional take on tea and snack time, *Guemokdang (pictured)* is a brick-clad blast from the past. Red bean is the house special, served chilled in the summer atop shaved ice or spooned over a wholesome bowl of porridge during winter.
• Various locations

Food | Milky Effervescence

Soju served in a signature green bottle may be widely known as the quintessential Korean alcohol, but some nationals might disagree—including the mother-son duo behind *Bogdeogbang*. With an emphasis on natural makgeolli, a fermented rice drink with a milky and effervescent texture, minus the usual chemicals, this charming eatery fashions homemade Korean dishes from locally sourced ingredients that pair perfectly with the drink. When ordering, tell the owner how many bottles of makgeolli you want to try and he will give recommendations.
• Bogdeogbang, 414-14 Mangwon 1(il)-dong, Mapo-gu

East Meets East

There's American-Chinese cuisine, with its fictitious generals and made-up names, and there's Korean-Chinese cuisine. Just as beloved as they are in the West, local iterations of Chinese flavours are a phenomenon worth experiencing. *Jin Jin* chef Yook-sung Wang took a gamble on this out-of-the-way location, but his high-quality cuisine and reasonable prices turned it into a win. Locals flock from all over Seoul to get a taste of dishes like his stir-fried king crab with egg whites, mushrooms and bamboo shoots. Book ahead to beat the queue.
• Jin Jin, 123 Jandari-ro, Seogyo-dong

Food **Plant Forward**

In the land of barbecued pork and chicken fried a million ways, vegan and vegetarian options may seem hard to come by. But *Sukara* has been providing hearty plant-based fare since 2006. The all-organic menu, fresh and straight from the garden, is crafted by a third-generation Korean-Japanese chef with roots in macrobiotic cuisine. Come with a few minutes to spare and check out the legendary Sanulrim Theater, located directly above the café. The historic venue was founded in 1985 and has spawned scores of national celebrities.
• Café Sukara, 157 Wausan-ro, Seogyo-dong, Mapo-gu

Night **Moonlighter**

As the epicentre of Seoul's cultural scene, Hongdae offers no shortage of live music venues. Few of them as beloved by artists and audiences alike as *Jebi Dabang*. Set up by an architect and designer duo who are also brothers, this place doubles as the headquarters for a record label, magazine publisher and architecture studio. Café by day and bar by night, drop in Thursday through Sunday to check out the latest live acts on the local indie scene. Space is tight so come early, and don't forget to drop a tip in the tin for the musicians before you leave.
• Jebi Dabang, 330-12, Sangsu-dong

Iconic Eats

The world's fastest internet connection may have helped South Koreans become the society with the highest index of online grocery shopping. But in recent years, young locals have begun flocking to *Mangwon Market* seeking a taste of the past. Blend in with the throngs of shoppers—young and old—and stroll about aimlessly while you take in seasonal produce, the sundry 'banchan' side dishes so essential to Korean cuisine and pantry staples. If the walk makes you hungry, indulge in a bowl of fried chicken bites doused with sweet sauce and deep-fried croquettes for just 500 won, or dine in at the market vendors' favourite knife-cut noodle shop for 3,000. Weather permitting, take your haul down to the Han River for a waterside picnic.

• Mangwon Market, 7 Mangwon-ro 8-gil, Mangwon 1(il)-dong, Mapo-gu

8,000   새우전   10,000   고추전   10,000   볼락
5,000   동태전   10,000   버섯전   10,000   돼지꼬리
0,000   깻잎전   10,000   머리고기(편육)
8,000   굴전   15,000   부추전   6,000   두부김치
5,000   5,000   골뱅이+소면
2,000   허파전   10,000   김치전

꼬막무침

Daniel Gray
He's the Korean foodie with a
hand in everything from tours to
consulting to establishments of
his own. Most recently featured
on a hit street food show, and
most likely to be found at a
market chowing down

Daniel Gray, Food Specialist

Taste Hunter

Daniel could sit and talk about food all night long. Throw some
kimchi and a dash of narcotic sauce in the mix and you've got the
makings of an epic evening. Here, the food expert dissects what it
is that makes Korean eating culture so great

What's your relationship with Seoul?

Well, I'm a Korean adoptee. I was born here and lived here until I was five. Then I was adopted by an American family, so I grew up in the United States. I returned because I wanted to find out about my roots—and I just found it to be a very fun and dynamic city and ended up staying. I would work as a teacher for a few months and then travel around for a couple of months and then come back. I learned the culture very quickly, and I was also accepted by different people very quickly. I was like a chameleon, people would notice I was different but not until they really got to know me. And then, because I was not really Korean, I was able to make friends quickly because I'm not subject to the same standards of social etiquette and decorum that other people are. Things like age, education, marital status, religion— all those things are very important within Korean society. And I was able to circumvent all that.

Can you tell us a little bit about your neighbourhood?

I live in the suburbs now with my family but I used to live in the Itaewon area, which was where the first North American style craft breweries started. It used to be a very expat-heavy area because it was close to the military base, which I could see from the window of my apartment. So there were Western restaurants, Korean restaurants, foreigners, locals. It was a big melting pot, just slightly more dangerous in comparison to the rest of Korea. Which isn't dangerous at all.

What is one smell that always reminds you of this city?

I would say more than a smell, it's like a feeling—the one I get when I think of something super clean like seaweed and cucumber soup. I don't even know if it has a real smell. I just like it. That feeling of freshness, crispness. A little bit of the sea, a little bit vinegary. Like a chilly breeze.

On the other end, I'd also say the smell of pork belly grease and kimchi, which is what I come home stinking of after the food tours I've been doing for ten years. By this point, it's embedded in my brain, second nature!

And what's the meal you miss the most when you're abroad?

I miss kimchi and fermented vegetables. I also miss my soup, my rice. I feel like a lot of western food tends to be too heavy. If I get a dish that's focused on meat, even though I enjoy eating it, I'll feel slow and sluggish afterwards. So I miss my pickles and my salads. When I'm travelling in Europe or America, if I can't get something like kimchi, I'll just ask for Tabasco sauce and lemon and dress a simple lettuce salad with that. That's my quick kimchi to balance out a meal.

The last few years have seen an explosion of Korean food on the international scene. But for now it's mostly bibimbap and barbecue. Can you give us a little run-down about what Korean food is really about?

I would say the bibimbap is quite representative of what Korean food is or can be. Not strictly the hot stone bowl, but definitely a mix of rice and different ingredients. What Korean restaurant food is really about, though, is what you can't make at home. Your mom can't cook it. You don't have a deep fryer, you don't have a bakery or a special coffee machine. So all the things you eat out are things you can't eat at home. But these barbecue places, what they do get right about Korean food culture is that they are places

Sometimes referred to as "The Republic of Fried Chicken", the savoury treat is never more than a few steps away

to host celebration meals. It's something that you do to socialise and celebrate. It's not strictly dinner per se, but it is the beginning of a great evening. That would be round one, and then you'd go for round two at a karaoke bar and then keep going. It's like a race, and it's all about being social and having things that you can do where you can get to know each other and share things. I think that's what makes Korean food very attractive.

What are some standout comfort food dishes and who makes your favourites in Seoul?

Galbitang would have to be one of my favourite dishes. It's like a beef rib soup, with green onion. You could have that with a bowl of hot rice and kkakdugi, which is the turnip kimchi, or regular cabbage kimchi. The beef is still on the bone,

and you take it off the bones—it makes for a very cosy, flavourful, wholesome meal. This is almost everywhere: the big roof house, *Kundyemanjik*, over by Nunghyan, *Nyeongdong*, a big restaurant next to the L7, and *Yetmat Seoul Bulgogi*. Only during lunch. Almost all good Korean barbecue places with have galbitang at lunchtime.

Where would you take someone who's hungry and just landed in town?

I usually like to go to the traditional Korean markets, Mangwon market or Gwangjang market, and do a tasting of all the different things so everyone can see the ingredients and learn about the foundation of how all the food is made. I'd make sure to include things like fried chicken or tteok-bokki, which are spicy rice cake noodles. There's always jjin mandu, steamed kimchi buns or pork buns. And hotteok, which are these caramel, cinnamon sugar donut things. Gwangjang market is a very iconic market, it's got the business and the right atmosphere. The things to get there would be the bindaettok, which are fried mung bean pancakes, at Yeumsoon Park's stall. Then there's mayak gimbap, which translates to "narcotic rice roll" because the sauce has spicy mustard, MSG, sugar, salt and soy sauce! Hard to stop eating those. And of course you have to go and eat the knife cut noodles there at *Yoongsun Cho*'s stall, along with the kimchi pancakes and kimchi dumplings and pork dumplings. A Korean would go to different places and chat and have a little here and there and keep going. Each place is never one whole meal, it's just a different stage for socialising. I would do many different rounds. There would definitely be some dak galbi, which is like a stir-fried spicy chicken with vegetables. I would go find that at *Nom Chuncheon Dakgalbi*.

Speaking of fried chicken! Where do we go?

I would probably just go to *Kyochon*, because they do it very well. Or I'd go to *Norangtungdack*. There's so much fried chicken everywhere, it's all about having it with beer. You can even get it delivered while sitting in a park somewhere. Fried chicken cup places are also great, like *Hong Cup* in Hongdae, which is a street food version of it.

Is there any new kind of cuisine or technique that Seoul is doing really well?

One of the big trends right now is what they call "K-Food". Following in the K-Beauty and K-Pop scenes. K-Food is basically taking a dish and exaggerating something about

it, making it into something Koreans would want. So a macaroon becomes a big giant pastry with lots of strawberries and things in the filling. It means putting lobster on a stick and covering it in cheese and blow-torching it or dipping very spicy ribs in cheese fondue. Just going above and beyond what should be acceptable as food. It's so over the top, it's actually great.

Three establishments in Seoul were recently awarded three Michelin stars, the highest honor for the guide. But there's been talk about whether or not they really qualify—what's your take on this? Is it really possible to measure kimchi against a universal marker of quality?

I will say one thing. I think in the first year, there shouldn't have been restaurants that already got three stars. Especially when those places haven't been around for very many years. I think that's a little suspect. Now, kimchi being on par with something like a truffle risotto, it's really hard to gauge because there's really, really good kimchi. But, it's alive! There's no way to get the consistent perfect kimchi every single time because it's always changing. Also, kimchi is not the main course of a meal. It's the accompaniment that balances things out. If you're just focusing on that, you might as well go to the best kimchi restaurant. But Koreans like their kimchi to come out to the table hot, and bubbling, and they like it very spicy and very sour. There's a very specific palate here. So, it's a difficult thing to judge.

Where would you take parents or in-laws for a fancy dinner?

It would be all about the ambience, so I would probably take them to what we call a hansik restaurant, which is a full-course Korean style restaurant. So you'll have a table

Nwijo offers a peaceful contrast to the street food scene with tables covered in small plates made for sharing

full of food: many different side dishes, meats, vegetables, fish, soups, everything just covering the whole table. Probably in a private room where you can have a private family conversation. So it's not so much focused on food as it is on the occasion, the people that you're with. Two places for this would be *Omiga* and Nwijo. Now, if I was with my in-laws, and I wanted to celebrate or impress them, I would take them to a nice buffet at a five-star hotel. Because the idea of having so much food and so much variety would be very impressive. And the thing about the way we eat is that it's still very social. So at the buffet, everyone would go on assignment to fetch different things for the whole table, instead of each one loading up their own plate.

You're also a family man—is there any place your kids are always excited to eat at?

We have these kids cafés, where the little ones can play and I have to say, the food at some of them is getting really good. There are some good ones by the *Lotte World Tower*, where there are aquariums. One is *Bounce Park*, but they're all over the place.

Kwangho Lee, Artist

Sideways Thinking

<u>Kwangho Lee</u>
He's an internationally-
acclaimed artist known for his
sculptural furniture, life-ready
art pieces and for blurring
the line between the two
categories

From styrofoam or straw to copper and electrical cord, there's no medium Lee won't work with. This spirit of exploration keeps the Seoul-based artist on the trail of his next big piece and his city's last great traditions

Where do you live in Seoul? What's it like?

I live on the northeastern periphery of Seoul—strictly speaking, on the border between Seoul and Gyeonggi-do province. My studio has always been in this city and I even grew up in an area near where I live now. Because it's on the fringe of the city, I've been able to experience both pastoral and urban life. Growing up, everything was in rapid development. I was surrounded by nature and yet just by turning around, I could see new apartments and residential complexes sprouting up.

How would you describe the city to someone who's never been?

It's a place where everything is blended seamlessly. New things are ready to be embraced and traditions are updated at a dizzying speed.

Where would you take visiting friends if they asked to go shopping and see beautiful things?

To the Hannam-Dong neighbourhood, also the hip Seongsu-Dong area with all its shops and cafés and finally to *Gyeongbokgung Palace*—a royal palace from the Joseon dynasty that dates back to 1395.

What are some of your favourite restaurants and what do you eat there?

I love Korean food—it's difficult to pick just one thing. I like to hang out with friends and creatives at *Manseon Hof*, I also frequent *Eulji Myeonok*, where I always get naengmyeon, cold buckwheat noodles, with soju.

Does Seoul influence your work?

It goes without saying. I have been working here for 12 years now. I make everything in Seoul and work and communicate with friends in Seoul. I believe I am deeply connected to this city.

Some of your work makes use of traditional Korean methods of craftsmanship—marrying them with very contemporary formats or subjects. Is there anywhere in Seoul that you think also does a great job of mixing the old with the new?

If we are only speaking of tradition, Insa-dong would be the right place. I am interested in the process of handling different materials and to do so, I consult with experts across various disciplines, which I enjoy. Similarly, you can witness the authentic mixture of the old and the new at the electronic components stores and manufacturing workshops around Euljiro-3-ga and Euljiro-4-ga.

Going back to tradition—where can we find a piece of traditional South Korea in Seoul?

I'm also trying to figure that out! I think I have yet to find it. The country strived to secure rapid growth after the Korean War, a process during which I believe we let the beauty we had slip away somehow. Seoul sometimes looks glamorous and trendy, but I'm also still in search of what it is that we had in the past—things that were also valuable.

Where do you always find inspiration within the city?

Each area has its own charms. But I do frequent Euljiro and Seongsu-dong, areas in which I naturally find inspiration.

If you could design one piece for Seoul, what would it be?

I would create a massive park with trees, grass, flowers and pebbles.

Mixed Media

BEAUTIFUL RIVERS AND MOUNTAINS:
THE PSYCHEDELIC ROCK SOUND
OF SOUTH KOREA'S
Shin Joong Hyun
1958–1974

신중현
아름다운 강산:
대한민국 신중현의 싸이키델릭 록 사운드

From Hendrixian to Motownesque, soulful and bluesy to upbeat and energetic, this compilation tells the musical tale of one of South Korea's most enigmatic rock legends. After building a transistor radio to snag the US Armed Forces Korean Network's jazz and rock broadcasts, musician and composer Shin Joong Hyun went on to introduce inquisitive South Korean masses to psychedelic rock and culture. But fame turned ugly when, after refusing to pen a song for president Park Chung-Hee and his ruling party, he was thrown in jail for possession of marijuana. After enduring torture, isolation and forced internment in a mental asylum, Shin eventually reemerged to cement his place in national music history. The story ends well—with a world-renowned body of work and a landmark performance in the USA, land of his dreams, as part of the Korean Music Festival at the Hollywood Bowl.
• Shin Joong Hyun, Beautiful Rivers and Mountains

Books

Pachinko
• Min Jin Lee, 2017

Delving into the historical ties between Japan and Korea, this novel features a large ensemble of characters in various social circumstances—spanning generations, countries and languages.

Please Look After Mom
• Shin Kyung-sook, 2011

Kyung-sook Shin's landmark novel, which sold one million copies within 10 months of its release, explores notions of loss, identity, self-discovery and gender roles.

The Vegetarian
• Han Kang, 2007

An artist and homemaker's life goes off the rails after she has a gruesome dream that spurs her to stop eating meat. Han Kang's three-part novel earned her a Man Booker award and international fame—all for a book deemed "very extreme and bizarre" by Korean audiences when it was originally published.

Films

Grass
• Hong Sang-soo, 2018

Hong Sang-soo's drama takes the notion of people-watching to the extreme, by way of a fascinating main character whose main pastime is to sit in the same Seoul café and use its guests' conversations as fodder for her own writing.

3-Iron
• Kim Ki-duk, 2004

Renowned director Kim Ki-duk offers up an unexpected and heartwarming story about a kind-hearted squatter and a housewife in need of sympathy.

Lady Vengeance
• Park Chan-wook, 2005

The third and final instalment in Park Chan-wook's dazzling Vengeance Trilogy, this film follows the story of a wrongly-incarcerated woman who manages to find freedom and sets out on a mission to take revenge on those who ruined her life.

Music

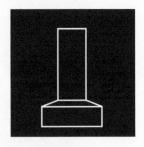

Second Language
• XXX, 2019

In a country where only K-pop darlings and reality TV show stars occupy the top of the charts, rapper-producer duo XXX's popularity makes them all the more impressive. Their second album is a cinematic undertaking, all caustic beats and ideological mumble.

Don't Mess Up My Tempo
• Exo, 2018

The sixth and best-selling studio album by "the world's greatest boy band" is a solid primer for those unfamiliar with the (global) phenomenon known as K-pop. The '90s may be back for most of us in the West, but in Korea, they've always been alive and well.

Adventure
• OOHYO, 2015

Think dreamy melodies and lyrics about post-heartbreak pizza and nostalgic cups of tea. OOHYO makes the kind of synth-happy indie pop that demands little and yet somehow manages to lift spirits. Like most of her subsequent work, her debut album is a sugar-coated ode to youth.

The Bando Hotel

Heinz Insu Fenkl

I don't know why I decided to walk from Chongro 3-ga through Insadong and down toward Euljiro and City Hall. Maybe it was just the beautiful day, the clear blue sky full of gentle, puffy clouds, or maybe the stiff, cool breeze had cleared the air of auto exhaust and the smell of boiling pig carcasses in the alley by the underground Hollywood Market, where I had just delivered an Omega watch. My mother owed a lot of money to Busy-Busy, the proprietor of one of the stalls, and was paying it off in black market goods. It had been a while since my last visit there, a year or so ago, and that time, underground, with everyone chain smoking in the humid heat, I could barely breathe as I hauled heavy shopping bags full of American canned goods. Now, outside and unburdened of some of my mother's debt, I felt like I could breathe freely. The people in the street seemed to have a brisk energy in their step, and even underneath, in the stifling Hollywood Market, the Yankee goods merchants had been in an unusually good mood—even Busy-Busy, whose cut wrists had healed, leaving another set of parallel tallies of how much money she was owed. With the U.S. Embassy nearby, you could see lots of foreigners in Insadong—mostly U.S. military and diplomatic corps—out shopping for antiques and celadon, or eating at the restaurants that made traditional foods to fit a foreign palate. One of the little tofu restaurants was a longtime hang-out, every other Thursday night, for spies, bankers, and members of the intelligence corps. The embassy workers and foreign pedestrians in Insadong dressed in the latest fashions unless they were in uniform, and the locals usually didn't make a big deal unless they happened to be blond women. I was wearing green and black striped velvet bell bottoms and a white Nehru shirt, and with my long hair, I would have attracted all sorts of attention in Bupyeong, but here I was, just part of the background. So when I heard shopkeepers exclaiming and pointing down the street, talking about a movie star named Oduri, I was curious. I couldn't figure out the name at first— Oduri sounded Japanese to me—but then, when a silk merchant said "Breakfast at Tiffany's," I realized they meant Audrey Hepburn. What would she be doing in Insadong? I thought, and I turned down the street in the direction everyone was pointing. She wasn't in Insadong. She'd already passed through and was a couple of blocks south, walking from the Chosun Hotel toward the Bando in her black dress and long black gloves, cat-eye sunglasses, and black kitten heels—Audrey Hepburn, or, more precisely, Holly Golightly. She even wore the earrings, pearl necklace, and tiara, and carried a long-stemmed cigarette holder from which she puffed every few steps as she adjusted her white scarf over her black handbag.

I expected to see George Peppard in his tweed jacket walking with her, or maybe a white paper bag and a cup of to-go coffee in her other hand. Drivers were pausing to rubberneck, and everyone was pointing and looking left and right to see if there might be a film crew down the block. I had to push past a small crowd of middle school girls in their school uniforms to get a closer look, excited, to my own surprise, that I might actually get to see a real movie star. But this was Audrey Hepburn, and that movie she was in must have been over a decade old, and what would she be doing in Seoul, near the embassy, dressed like Holly Golightly?

There was no camera crew on the street, though some people with cameras were snapping pictures of her, and when I got close enough into that strange empty zone where no one seemed bold enough to approach, I saw that it wasn't Audrey Hepburn at all. She wore only three strands of pearls, her black dress was cut shorter, and the highlights in her hair, above the tiara, were the wrong color. It was Patsy McCabe. And then I felt strange—thrilled in a different way than to see a movie star, but also physically sick, as if I had seen something like a terrible car accident.

Everyone was saying "Audrey! Audrey!" so when I called out to her by her real name, she stumbled and turned to look.

She tried to cover up by pretending she was only ashing her cigarette.

"Patsy!" I called again.

This time she saw me, and made a curt gesture with her head toward the entrance of the Bando Hotel. The doorman held the door open for her and she quickly went inside. I followed in a moment, past the doorman's disapproving once-over. Patsy stood by the couches near the concierge, and in the muted light of the hotel lobby she looked like Audrey Hepburn again. A Korean man in an expensive navy suit approached her and they exchanged a few words I couldn't make out. Patsy pointed in my direction and the man looked at me, nodded, and gave a small bow before walking away to attend to other patrons. I heard him call her "Miss Audrey." "Patsy?" I said again. I hardly knew what to add after that. What else could I have said to her that wouldn't have been obvious or sarcastic? I couldn't see her eyes, but even behind those Manhattan sunglasses I could imagine her expression—a mixture of embarrassment and defiance—and so what she did was all the more surprising.

Patsy lowered her sunglasses, and looking over the rims at me, she took a puff of her cigarette and said, "My darling Fred! What brings you to the Bando?" I couldn't tell if she was putting me on or just trying to stay in character. Or maybe she had gone insane since I had seen her last. Fred was Holly Golightly's brother from back home in the boonies of Tulip, Texas. "What are you doing?" I said. She walked up to me and took my hand, leading me toward the elevators.

"What the fuck are you doing, Seven?" she said out of the side of her mouth, calling me by my nickname.

It was Patsy now—she even walked like Patsy in a way that seemed strangely inappropriate for her dress. We took the elevator up to the top floor and I followed her down a slightly musty hallway to what I guessed was her room. Patsy put the cigarette holder in her mouth so she could open her handbag for the room key, and when she bent over to insert it into the lock, the cigarette broke against the door. The tip burned a little black circle into the wood before it fell onto the carpet. I stepped on it.

"Fuck," said Patsy. She opened the door and we went inside.

Heinz Insu Fenkl is an award-winning author, editor, translator and folklorist. He is also an expert on North Korean comics and literature.

Also available from LOST iN

... and Austin, Dusseldorf, Edinburgh, Helsinki, Oslo, Porto, Reykjavik, Rotterdam, Seattle, Tangier, Tel Aviv in the LOST iN Mobile App.

LOSTIN.COM